ECIA Chapter 2

DE LA
3455
Chicago, IL 60616

362.1
OPH    AIDS
c.2

| DATE DUE | BORROWER'S NAME | ROOM NUMBER |
|---|---|---|
|  |  |  |
|  |  |  |
|  |  |  |
|  |  |  |
|  |  |  |
|  |  |  |

362.1
OPH    AIDS
c.2

LIBRARY
DE LA SALLE INSTITUTE
3455 So. Wabash Ave.
Chicago, Ill. 60616

# AIDS

## Distinguishing Between Fact and Opinion

# AIDS

## Distinguishing Between Fact and Opinion

**Curriculum Consultant: JoAnne Buggey, Ph.D.**
College of Education, University of Minnesota

**By Teresa Opheim**

**OPPOSING JUNIORS VIEWPOINTS**

Greenhaven Press, Inc.
Post Office Box 289009
San Diego, CA 92198-0009

**Titles in the opposing viewpoints juniors series:**

Smoking            Death Penalty
Gun Control        Drugs and Sports
Animal Rights      Toxic Wastes
AIDS               Patriotism
Alcohol            Working Mothers
Immigration        Terrorism

Cover photo: R. Felman/National Institutes of Health

**Library of Congress Cataloging-in-Publication Data**

Opheim, Teresa.
    AIDS, distinguishing between fact and opinion / by Teresa Opheim; curriculum consultant. JoAnne Buggey.
        p.   cm. — (Opposing viewpoints juniors)
    Summary: Opposing viewpoints discuss such issues concerning AIDS as how it is spread and whether it is a moral issue.
    ISBN 0-89908-633-0
    1. AIDS (Disease)—Moral and ethical aspects—Juvenile literature.
    2. AIDS (Disease)—Social aspects—Juvenile literature.    3. Critical thinking—Juvenile literature.    [1. AIDS (Disease)]  I. Title.
    II. Series.
    RC607.A26064 1989
    362.1'969792—dc20                                             89-12006
                                                                    CIP
                                                                    AC

No part of this book may be reproduced or used in any other form or by any other means, electrical, mechanical or otherwise, including, but not limited to photocopy, recording or any information storage and retrieval system, without prior written permission from the publisher.

Copyright 1989 by Greenhaven Press, Inc.

# CONTENTS

The Purpose of This Book: **An Introduction to Opposing Viewpoints**..................6
Skill Introduction: **What Is the Difference Between Fact and Opinion?**.........7
Sample Viewpoint A: **AIDS is everyone's problem**..................................8
Sample Viewpoint B: **AIDS is not everyone's problem**.............................9
Analyzing the
Sample Viewpoints: **Tallying the Facts and Opinions**...............................10

## Chapter 1

**Preface: Can AIDS Be Spread by Casual Contact?**........................11
Viewpoint 1: **AIDS might be spread by casual contact**.......................12
  paraphrased views of *Max Klinghoffer*
Viewpoint 2: **AIDS cannot be spread by casual contact**......................14
  paraphrased views of *J.W. Anderson*
Critical Thinking Skill 1: **Tallying the Facts and Opinions**.....................16

## Chapter 2

**Preface: Should the Food and Drug Administration Make AIDS Drugs More Available?**......................................................17
Viewpoint 3: **The FDA should make AIDS drugs more available**..........18
  paraphrased views of *Mathilde Krim*
Viewpoint 4: **The FDA should not make AIDS drugs more available**...20
  paraphrased views of *Daniel S. Greenberg*
Critical Thinking Skill 2: **Distinguishing Between Fact and Opinion**....22

## Chapter 3

**Preface: Is AIDS a Moral Issue?**........................................................23
Viewpoint 5: **AIDS is a moral issue**......................................................24
  paraphrased views of *James K. Fitzpatrick*
Viewpoint 6: **AIDS is not a moral issue**................................................26
  paraphrased views of *Alan M. Dershowitz*
Critical Thinking Skill 3: **Analyzing AIDS Advertising**........................28

**Glossary of Terms**................................................................................31

# THE PURPOSE OF THIS BOOK

## An Introduction to Opposing Viewpoints

When people disagree, it is hard to figure out who is right. You may decide one person is right just because the person is your friend or relative. But this is not a very good reason to agree or disagree with someone. It is better if you try to understand why these people disagree. On what main points do they differ? Read or listen to each person's argument carefully. Separate the facts and opinions that each person presents. Finally, decide which argument best matches what you think. This process, examining an argument without emotion, is part of what critical thinking is all about.

This is not easy. Many things make it hard to understand and form opinions. People's values, age, and experience all influence the way they think. This is why learning to read and think critically is an invaluable skill. Opposing Viewpoints Juniors books will help you learn and practice skills to improve your ability to read critically. By reading opposing views on an issue, you will become familiar with methods people use to attempt to convince you that their point of view is right. And you will learn to separate the authors' opinions from the facts they present.

Each Opposing Viewpoints Juniors book focuses on one critical thinking skill that will help you judge the views presented. Some of these skills are telling fact from opinion, recognizing propaganda techniques, and locating and analyzing the main idea. These skills will allow you to examine opposing viewpoints more easily.

Each viewpoint in this book is paraphrased from the original to make it easier to read. The viewpoints are placed in a running debate and are always placed with the pro view first.

## SKILL INTRODUCTION

# What Is the Difference Between Fact and Opinion?

In this Opposing Viewpoints Juniors book you will be asked to identify and study statements of fact and statements of opinion. A fact is a statement that can be proved true. Here are some examples of factual statements: "The Statue of Liberty was dedicated in 1886 in New York," "Dinosaurs are extinct," and "George Washington was the first U.S. President." It is fairly easy to prove these facts true. For instance, a historian in the year 3000 might need to prove when the Statue of Liberty was dedicated. One way she might do this is to check in the Hall of Records in New York. She would try to find a source such as a newspaper article, the mayor's speech, or a picture of the dedication plaque to verify the date. Sometimes it is harder to check facts. In this book you will be asked to question facts in the viewpoints, and you will be given some ways in which you might go about proving them.

Statements of opinion cannot be proved. An opinion expresses how a person feels about something or what a person thinks is true. Remember the facts we mentioned? They can easily be changed into statements of opinion. For example, "Dinosaurs became extinct because a huge meteor hit the Earth," "George Washington was the best president the United States ever had," and "Rebuilding the Statue of Liberty was a waste of money," are all statements of opinion. They express what one person believes to be true. Opinions are not better than facts. They are different. Opinions are based on many things, including religious, moral, social, and family values. Opinions can also be based on medical and scientific facts. For instance, many scientists have made intelligent guesses about other planets based on what they know is true about earth. The only way these scientists would know their opinions were right is if they were able to visit other planets and test their guesses. Until their guesses are proved, then, they remain opinions. Some people have opinions that we do not like, or with which we disagree. That does not always make their opinions wrong, or right. There is room in our world for many different opinions.

When you read differing views on any issue, it is very important to know when people are using facts and when they are using opinions in an argument. When writers use facts, their arguments are more believable and easier to prove. The more facts the author uses, the more the reader can tell that the writer's opinion is based on something other than personal feelings.

Arguments that are based mostly on the author's opinions are impossible to prove factually true. This does not mean these types of arguments are not important. It means that you, as the reader, must decide whether or not you agree or disagree based on personal reasons, not factual ones.

We asked two students to give their opinions on the AIDS issue. Examine the following viewpoints. Look for facts and opinions in their arguments.

# SAMPLE VIEWPOINT A *Chris*

## AIDS is everyone's problem.

Reports say that more and more people are dying from AIDS all the time. Someday I think we're all going to know someone who has AIDS, the disease is spreading so fast. Also, the disease is so new, I think maybe you can get it more easily than the experts think.

Most of the people who have AIDS are gays and drug users, but that doesn't mean the rest of us shouldn't worry. People have gotten AIDS from blood transfusions, and babies have gotten it from their mothers who had AIDS. Also, my health teacher says that more people who aren't gay are getting it from having sex with someone who's infected.

Even if all the victims were gays and drug users, so what? If people are dying of a disease, we should care no matter who the victims are.

## SAMPLE VIEWPOINT B *Natasha*

### AIDS is not everyone's problem.

Homosexuals and drug users are the ones who get AIDS. We're not at risk if we stay away from those kinds of people.

And we should stay away from those kinds of people. Homosexuality is a sin. The Bible says it is, and everyone I know thinks it is. On top of that, gays often have sex with lots of different people, so they're responsible for spreading their own disease.

AIDS should make gays clean up their lifestyle. My father thinks that maybe AIDS is God's way of punishing gay people.

# ANALYZING THE SAMPLE VIEWPOINTS

Chris and Natasha have very different opinions about AIDS. Both of them use examples of fact and opinion in their arguments:

## Chris:

**FACTS**

More people are dying of AIDS all the time.

Not all AIDS victims are gay or drug users.

**OPINIONS**

AIDS will spread very fast.

AIDS is spread more easily than experts think.

## Natasha:

**FACTS**

The Bible says homosexuality is a sin.

AIDS affects homosexuals and drug users.

**OPINIONS**

Homosexuality is a sin.

AIDS should make gays clean up their lifestyles.

In this sample, Chris and Natasha both have an equal number of facts and opinions. Look at the opinions listed in this sample. Which opinions are based on religious or moral values and which are based on medical or scientific facts? Chris's opinions are based on scientific or medical information he knows about AIDS. On the other hand, Natasha's opinions are based on her religious and moral values.

Both Chris and Natasha think that they are right about AIDS. What conclusions would you come to from this sample? Why? Think of two facts and two opinions that you have about AIDS. As you continue to read through the viewpoints in this book, try keeping a tally like the one above to compare the authors' arguments.

# CHAPTER 1

## PREFACE: Can AIDS Be Spread by Casual Contact?

AIDS (Acquired Immune Deficiency Syndrome) is fatal. The AIDS virus attacks the body's immune system, which helps the body resist diseases. People who have AIDS can get other diseases more easily because their immune systems are weak. They often die from diseases such as pneumonia, which usually is not fatal to a person who does not have AIDS.

AIDS is contagious, meaning it is spread by contact. But what kind of contact is required? Many experts believe that the AIDS virus is passed from one person to another mostly through sexual contact, blood transfusions, and dirty needles used by intravenous drug users. Intravenous, or IV, drug users use needles to take drugs.

But a few people believe that AIDS may also be spread by casual contact such as touching the same food or using the same bathroom. These people argue that society must isolate people with AIDS and not allow them to work in restaurants, hospitals, and schools. In the next two viewpoints, the authors debate whether this is necessary. The first author says that AIDS carriers should not be hired to work in public places such as restaurants and schools. He argues this because he believes AIDS may be spread by casual contact. The second author argues that AIDS probably is not spread by casual contact. He concludes that AIDS carriers should not be kept from working in restaurants and hospitals just because they have AIDS.

When reading these viewpoints, use your critical reading skills to find the facts and opinions each author presents. Which case is more strongly based on fact, or are they equally factual?

## VIEWPOINT 1

# AIDS might be spread by casual contact

**Editor's Note:** This viewpoint was paraphrased from an article by Max Klinghoffer, a medical doctor. In it, Dr. Klinghoffer argues that there are a lot of things about AIDS that experts do not understand. Dr. Klinghoffer says that experts should not argue that AIDS cannot be spread by casual contact until they know more about how the disease is spread.

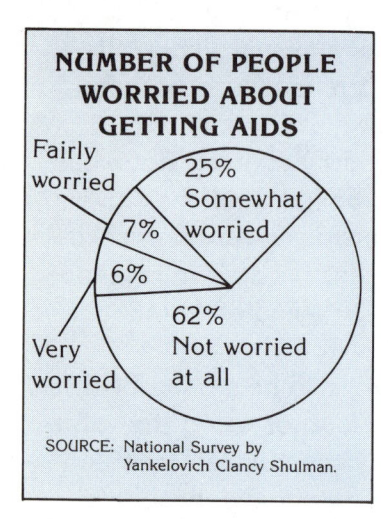

**NUMBER OF PEOPLE WORRIED ABOUT GETTING AIDS**

- Fairly worried: 7%
- Somewhat worried: 25%
- Very worried: 6%
- Not worried at all: 62%

SOURCE: National Survey by Yankelovich Clancy Shulman.

**Is the author's conclusion based on fact or opinion?**

**The author raises a series of questions here. Does he provide any answers?**

Can the AIDS virus be spread by casual contact? Most researchers think the answer is no. They cite statistics that show that few or none of the people in close contact with AIDS patients have gotten AIDS. From these few studies, these experts conclude that AIDS is not contracted through casual contact with an infected person.

But the researchers have reached a conclusion—a deadly important conclusion—without sufficient scientific evidence. The incubation period, the time that the AIDS virus is kept in the body before it becomes active, may be several years. It might take up to fourteen years from the time a person contracts AIDS to the time the virus becomes active.

We found out about this disease in 1981. It will be 1995 before we will find out if those who had casual contact with AIDS victims in 1981 will get the disease or not. Right now, AIDS is too new for us to be able to decide for sure how people catch it.

The media have given us a lot of information about AIDS. We are told that blood transfusions are now safe because available tests tell us whether the donor does or does not have AIDS. But what happens if a donor has just recently been exposed to the AIDS virus, but his tests for the virus are still negative? He donates blood, but a month later he finds out he has AIDS. What do we now tell those who received that blood? Is an apology sufficient for a death sentence?

There has been a lot of talk about controlling AIDS. This talk has been focused on educating people who are at risk and on preventing the spread of AIDS. This is not enough. The government must get involved before the epidemic is out of control.

The government should not allow AIDS patients to be food handlers. It should not allow AIDS victims to be in jobs caring for children, nor should they be in hospital work that brings them into contact with other individuals. These regulations should apply unless we find out *beyond any doubt* that AIDS cannot be spread by these kinds of contacts.

Strong steps must be taken at once or the majority of our population may get the AIDS virus. If not, we shall all become unwilling characters in Edgar Allan Poe's story, *The Masque of the Red Death*. The first two sentences of the story read: "The 'Red Death' had long devastated the country. No pestilence had ever been so fatal or so hideous." The story concludes: "And darkness and decay and the Red Death held dominion over all."

**The author's conclusion is very bleak. What does he think will happen if we are not more cautious about AIDS? Is this conclusion a fact or an opinion?**

Steve Kelley. Reprinted with permission.

### Do we have enough proof?

Dr. Klinghoffer would not allow AIDS patients to be food handlers until we find out beyond any doubt that AIDS cannot be spread by casual contact. Do you agree with Dr. Klinghoffer?

# VIEWPOINT 2 AIDS cannot be spread by casual contact

**Editor's Note:** This viewpoint is paraphrased from an article by J.W. Anderson, a writer for the *Washington Post*. In it, Mr. Anderson discusses two studies that support his view that AIDS is not spread by casual contact.

**How could you prove these facts are true?**

**Is this first sentence a fact or an opinion?**

**How many facts are in this paragraph? How many opinions?**

AIDS is a terrible disease—painful and, so far, fatal. It also is contagious. As it spreads, important questions arise about controlling it.

More than 22,600 cases of AIDS have been diagnosed so far in this country. Ninety-five percent of the victims fall into these three categories: homosexuals, babies whose mothers were infected, and people who got the disease from needle injections or blood transfusions.

How did the other 5 percent get AIDS? Some died before doctors could answer this question. Some were small children who probably got the disease from transfusions.

We cannot prove that you can get AIDS only from the ways mentioned above—sexual contact, blood transfusions, and birth. But the most important evidence we have about how the disease is spread is the studies of who did and who did not get the virus.

Dr. Gerald H. Friedland and others at Montefiore Medical Center in the Bronx, New York, have been carefully studying 145 people who have had close contact with people who have AIDS. These people were not sexual partners of the victims, but many shared kitchens and bathrooms with the AIDS patients. They hugged the patients and helped them bathe and eat. Seven even shared toothbrushes with them.

Out of the 145, only one tested positive for the AIDS virus. She is the five-year-old daughter of two drug addicts, both infected. She probably got the disease at birth from her mother.

Another report studied three hundred doctors, nurses, and orderlies who work with AIDS patients in hospitals. These health care workers had close contact with AIDS patients for nearly four years. The study, published in the *New England Journal of Medicine*, found that of the three hundred, all tested negative for the AIDS virus except for fourteen who were homosexuals.

There are only two known cases in which hospital workers have become infected with the AIDS virus. Both were accidentally injected with the infected blood of an AIDS victim.

These studies come to the same point: There are only three known ways to get AIDS—sexual contact, blood transfusions, and birth. That is why public health officials have concluded that people cannot get AIDS through normal daily contact at school or at work.

Society has the power to isolate people who carry dangerous diseases. But AIDS victims should not be isolated just because other people fear them.

AIDS carriers should not be kept from jobs in schools, restaurants, and offices. There is no evidence of an AIDS carrier who got the disease through the normal contacts of daily life.

**What do these facts prove about AIDS? Do you think there is much danger of catching AIDS after reviewing these facts?**

**Is the author's conclusion a fact or an opinion? Do you agree or disagree?**

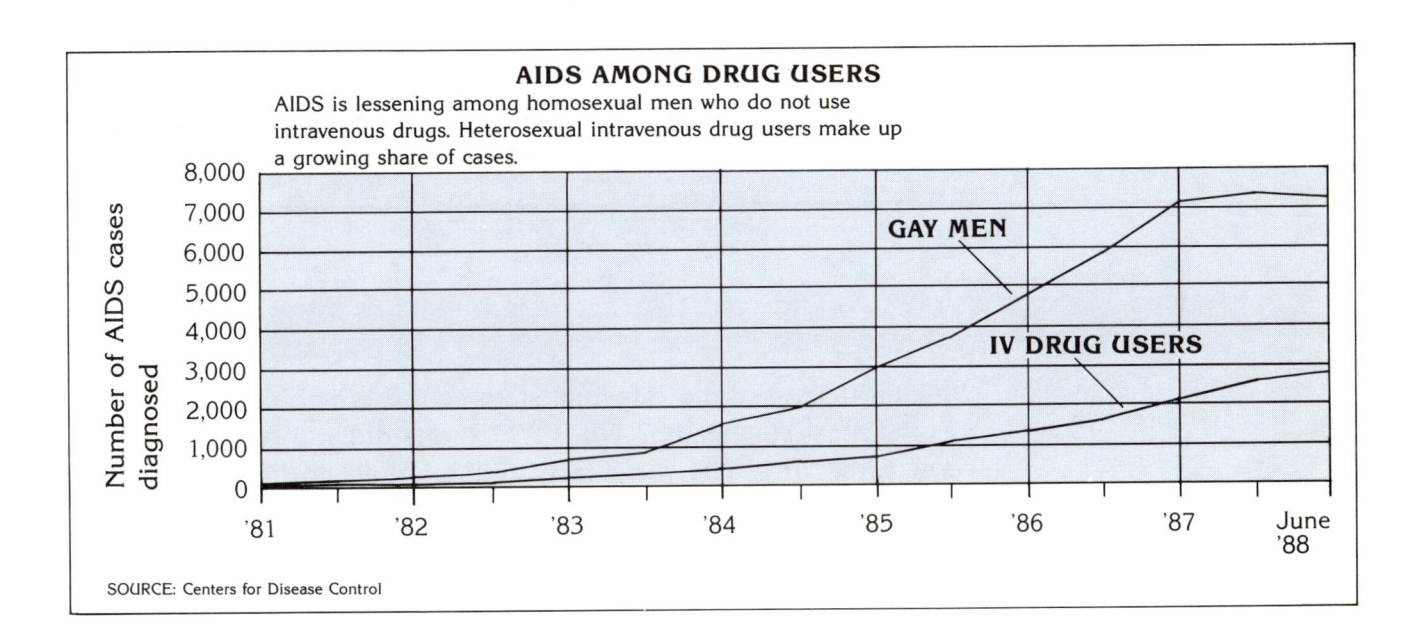

**AIDS AMONG DRUG USERS**

AIDS is lessening among homosexual men who do not use intravenous drugs. Heterosexual intravenous drug users make up a growing share of cases.

Number of AIDS cases diagnosed

GAY MEN

IV DRUG USERS

'81  '82  '83  '84  '85  '86  '87  June '88

SOURCE: Centers for Disease Control

### How is AIDS spread?

Mr. Anderson cites two studies to support his argument that AIDS victims should be allowed to work in schools, restaurants, and offices. What do you conclude from these studies? Do you think they prove Mr. Anderson's argument?

## CRITICAL THINKING SKILL 1
### Tallying the Facts and Opinions

After reading the two viewpoints on whether AIDS is spread by casual contact, make a chart similar to the one made for Chris and Natasha on page 10. List the facts and opinions each author gives to make his case. A chart is started for you below:

## Anderson:

**FACTS**

More than 22,600 cases of AIDS have been diagnosed so far in this country.

**OPINIONS**

Existing studies are the most important evidence we have about how AIDS is spread.

## Klinghoffer:

**FACTS**

Incubation period for AIDS may be several years.

**OPINIONS**

The government must get involved before the epidemic is out of control.

Which article used more factual statements? Which did you think was the most convincing? Why? Which one did you personally agree with? Why? List some facts and opinions, not in the articles, that have influenced your opinion about AIDS.

# CHAPTER 2

## PREFACE: Should the Food and Drug Administration Make AIDS Drugs More Available?

In the United States, all drugs must be approved by a government organization called the Food and Drug Administration, or FDA. The FDA tests drugs to make sure they are safe and effective for the people who take them. In the case of AIDS, most scientists think it will be years before there is a vaccine or cure for AIDS. In the meantime, many experimental, or unapproved, drugs are being tested. Some of the drugs seem to help AIDS victims. But the FDA says more tests are required before it can determine that the drugs are safe and effective.

The FDA tests drugs for years before the drugs can be released. This is partly because drugs were released in the past that later caused major illness or death. Since then, the FDA has become much more careful, approving drugs only when it is certain that the drugs are safe.

The tough testing process helps keep dangerous drugs away from the public. It also means patients may not get a hopeful new drug that could save their lives.

In the next two viewpoints, the authors debate whether patients should be allowed to get experimental AIDS drugs before the drugs are approved by the FDA. The first author concludes that the FDA should make the experimental drugs more available to people who are very sick. The second author concludes that making these experimental drugs available might hurt the chances of finding a cure for AIDS.

When reading these two viewpoints, use your skills to find the facts and opinions each author presents. Are both viewpoints equally based on facts?

# VIEWPOINT 3 — The FDA should make AIDS drugs more available

**Editor's Note:** This viewpoint was paraphrased from an article written by Mathilde Krim, a research biologist at St. Luke's/Roosevelt Hospital Center and Columbia University's College of Physicians and Surgeons, both in New York. In it, Dr. Krim argues that experimental AIDS drugs should be given to AIDS patients who are about to die, even if the drugs have not been proven effective.

**Does the author start her viewpoint with a fact or an opinion?**

We need to provide treatment for AIDS patients who are dying. We should allow more AIDS patients to take experimental drugs.

The Food and Drug Administration (FDA) oversees the procedure for approving drugs. This procedure is cautious and time consuming. It protects citizens from drugs that would do more harm than good.

But the FDA does make some exceptions in its procedures. Some cancer drugs are released without FDA approval. But scientists must show at what dosage, or amount of the drug given, the drug is unsafe for the patient. They must show also that there is some reason to think the drug will fight the disease. These factors are balanced against how serious the disease will become if it is not treated.

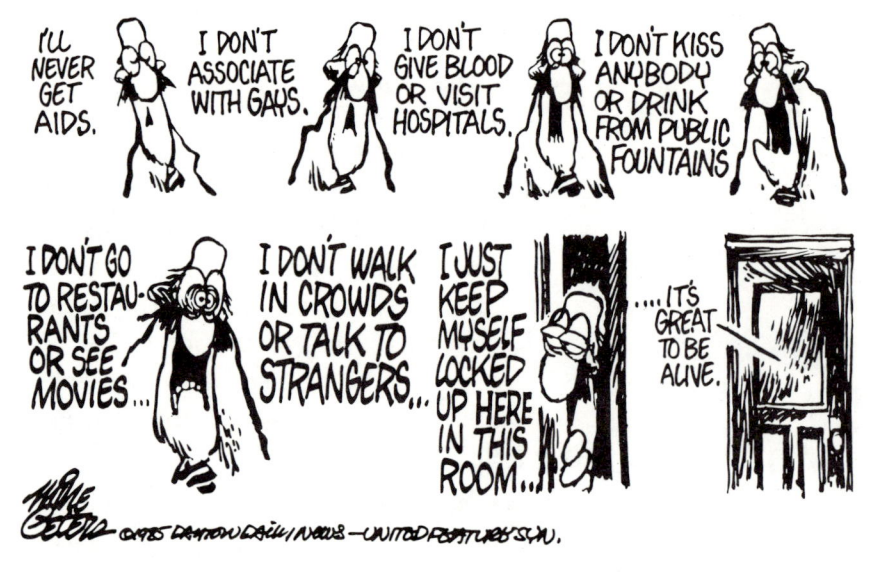

Mike Peters. Reprinted by permission of UFS., Inc.

18 JUNIORS

Currently, AIDS victims must be enrolled by medical doctors and researchers in carefully controlled studies at medical centers to receive experimental drugs. Only 10 percent of AIDS patients can hope to be accepted into these studies.

The studies cost more than ten thousand dollars a year for each patient. To make experimental drugs available to eighteen thousand patients would be very expensive—more than 180 million dollars in the first year. Also, the studies often are conducted at places that are far away from the patients' homes.

As a result, 90 percent of AIDS patients do not receive experimental treatment. As the number of AIDS cases increases, as it surely will, the proportion of AIDS patients accepted into these studies can only decrease.

Patients with cancer have hope because they can get treatment, even if the treatment is still experimental. Patients who have AIDS should be given the same hope. It has been said: "Without hope, the heart does break." As things stand now, the heart does break.

**Is this paragraph stating facts or opinions? How can you tell?**

**Why aren't more AIDS victims receiving treatment?**

**What does the author think would give AIDS victims hope?**

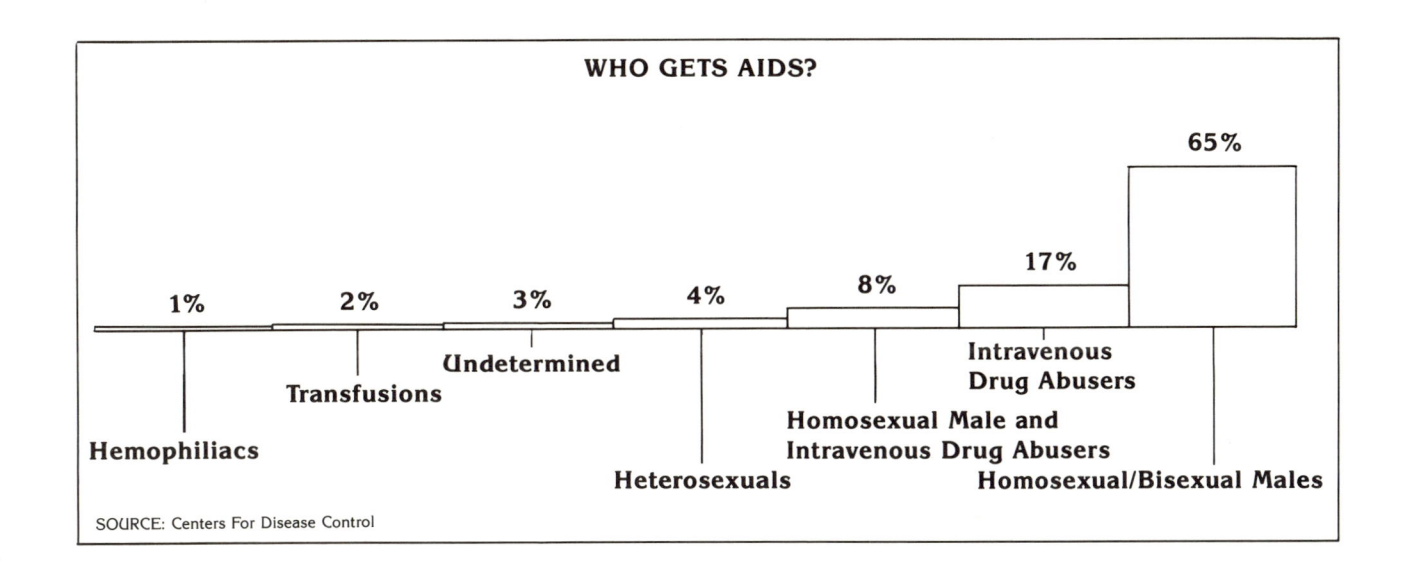

**WHO GETS AIDS?**

- 1% Hemophiliacs
- 2% Transfusions
- 3% Undetermined
- 4% Heterosexuals
- 8% Homosexual Male and Intravenous Drug Abusers
- 17% Intravenous Drug Abusers
- 65% Homosexual/Bisexual Males

SOURCE: Centers For Disease Control

**AIDS victims' last hope?**

List three facts and three opinions that the author gives to prove her view that experimental drugs should be made available to more AIDS patients.

## VIEWPOINT 4: The FDA should not make AIDS drugs more available

**Editor's Note:** This viewpoint was paraphrased from an article written by Daniel S. Greenberg, the publisher and editor of the periodical, *Science and Government Report,* and a columnist on science and health policy. In it, Mr. Greenberg argues that the FDA is not helping AIDS victims by letting them use untested, possibly harmful or useless, drugs.

AIDS patients are going to die anyway. Why not let them have any medicine that might possibly help?

The FDA has now answered that question. On March 10, 1987, the FDA announced that doctors could give experimental drugs to very sick AIDS patients. The FDA will allow this even if tests on the drugs are incomplete.

The FDA's intent is good, and it fulfills the public's desire to do everything we possibly can to stop AIDS. But early release of new drugs will make the problem worse rather than solve it.

None of these experimental drugs has worked very well so far. Some of the drugs, however, do delay death for some patients.

**Are the author's criticisms based on fact or opinion? How can you tell?**

We need experimental drugs to be tested many times to solve the AIDS crisis. Without many tests, we do not know if some drugs allow AIDS patients to live healthier longer or merely stretch out their painful deaths. Only careful tests on the drugs and dosage levels will prove this.

It is easy to be impatient with the slow-moving FDA. But the FDA is slow because it must sort out sick people's reactions to these complicated chemicals. Allowing the use of unproved and perhaps unsafe drugs is just too dangerous.

By permission of Johnny Hart and NAS, Inc. (The Wizard of Id)

Dr. Martin Hirsch of Massachusetts General Hospital has stated that it is impossible to conduct tests on how safe and effective a drug is when the drug is released early. We should try instead, Hirsch said, to do more trials of drugs on patients.

Indeed, more and more drugs and patients are being used in experiments. The process is slow, but it is the only way to make safe drugs available. Hasty approval of unproved drugs is not the answer.

**Are Hirsch's statements facts or opinions?**

**Do you agree with the author's conclusions? Why or why not?**

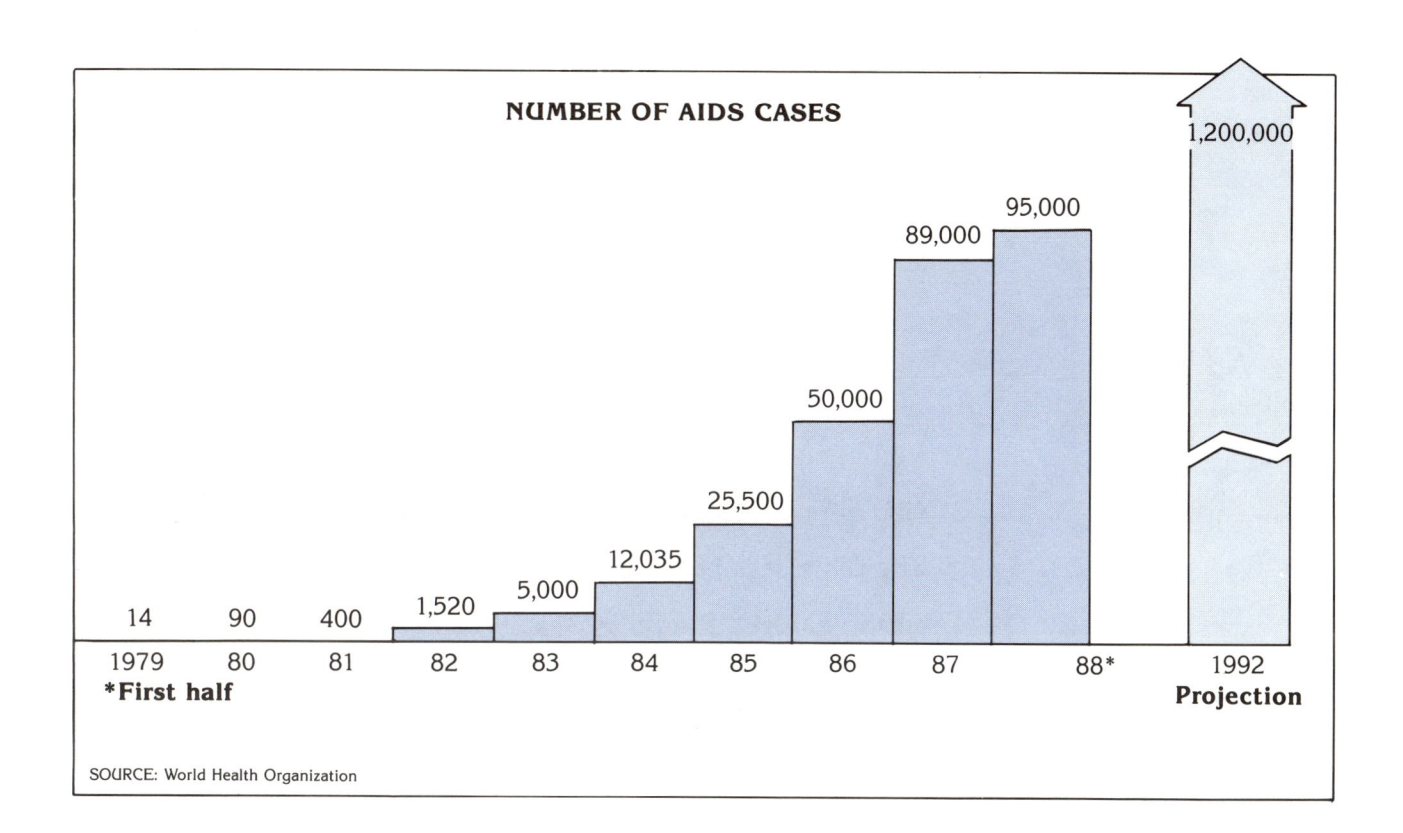

**NUMBER OF AIDS CASES**

| Year | Cases |
|---|---|
| 1979 | 14 |
| 80 | 90 |
| 81 | 400 |
| 82 | 1,520 |
| 83 | 5,000 |
| 84 | 12,035 |
| 85 | 25,500 |
| 86 | 50,000 |
| 87 | 89,000 |
| 88* | 95,000 |
| 1992 Projection | 1,200,000 |

*First half

SOURCE: World Health Organization

### How much proof?

List three facts and three opinions that the author gives to prove his view that experimental drugs should not be given to more AIDS patients.

AIDS **21**

## CRITICAL THINKING SKILL 2

# Distinguishing Between Fact and Opinion

This activity will allow you to practice distinguishing between fact and opinion. The statements below focus on the subject matter of this chapter, whether or not AIDS is a moral issue. Read each statement and consider it carefully. *Mark O for any statement you believe is an opinion, or what one person believes to be true. Mark F for any statement you believe is a fact, or something that can be proven to be true. Mark U for any statement for which you cannot decide.*

If you are doing this activity as a member of a class or group, compare your answers with other class or group members. You will find that others may have different answers than you do. Listening to the reasons others give for their answers can help you in distinguishing fact from opinion.

**EXAMPLE:** AIDS victims do not deserve our sympathy. It's their own fault that they have the disease.

**ANSWER:** O, opinion. AIDS victims may or may not deserve our sympathy, but it cannot be proven. This statement is one person's opinion.

*Answer*

1. Homosexuals are the only ones affected by AIDS. _____

2. God is punishing homosexuals with AIDS. _____

3. The Bible says homosexuality is wrong. _____

4. AIDS is mostly spread by sexual contact and IV drug use. _____

5. AIDS can be prevented. _____

6. Scientists are still discovering new information about AIDS. _____

7. There is no cure for AIDS. _____

8. People who believe AIDS is a punishment for homosexuals are nuts. _____

# CHAPTER 3

## PREFACE: Is AIDS a Moral Issue?

Because AIDS affects homosexuals, it is not just a health issue in many people's minds. Many people see AIDS as a moral issue as well. Morality involves the conduct that your community and family think is right. Morality is often, but not always, based on religious beliefs.

Those who think homosexuality is immoral and those who do not disagree over what should be done about AIDS. They disagree about how easily the disease is spread. They disagree about what, if any, restrictions should be placed on homosexual behavior.

In the next two arguments, you will read the views of two people who disagree about whether AIDS is a moral issue. As you read the viewpoints, look for the facts and opinions that each author presents. Then examine these facts and opinions to see if they have a moral or religious basis.

# VIEWPOINT 5  AIDS is a moral issue

**Editor's Note:** This viewpoint was paraphrased from an article written by James K. Fitzpatrick, a free-lance writer. In it, Mr. Fitzpatrick claims that AIDS is not merely a medical problem, as many claim, but a moral problem.

**Is this second sentence a fact or an opinion?**

**How many facts and how many opinions are in this paragraph?**

**Is this a fact or an opinion? How would you prove that this was true?**

Some have tried to convince us that there is not a moral part to AIDS. They do not think we need to think morally about how much time, energy, and sympathy society owes to AIDS victims.

Only in private can you discuss the idea that homosexuals have some role to play in stopping the spread of AIDS. Many think that it is society's responsibility to find a cure so homosexuals can continue their "lifestyle."

On radio call-in shows, I have heard homosexuals assure us that God could not will that homosexuals get AIDS. Yet they then attack their critics who say that God *could* will such a punishment. It seems God can have a voice in public opinion only if He agrees with the homosexuals and their supporters.

Should Christians see AIDS as the will of God? It is hard to see how one could conclude that, because there is no way to know the will of God. But one thing is certain: Near to 75 percent of those who get the disease are homosexuals.

And the other 25 percent are indirectly related to homosexuals. The drug users used a needle once used by a homosexual. Others received a blood transfusion from a homosexual. The disease is being spread by homosexuals to each other and more and more to the rest of society.

Those who are responsible for the AIDS outbreak are men and women who are engaging in acts that have been defined as sinful by the Judeo-Christian community for two thousand years. Most other societies think of homosexuality as sinful as well. Warnings, punishments, scorn, and prayer have been used to try to end homosexual behavior.

Homosexuals have chosen to ignore all this. For them, the Bible is wrong, the church is wrong, society is wrong. Their sexual activity is not a sin.

24   JUNIORS

Indeed, some members of homosexual groups are displeased when other homosexuals call for an end to numerous sexual partners and casual pickups. Limiting themselves to one or two "safe" partners is too great a price to pay. One New York "gay" complained in a *New York Times* interview that "safe sex is unexciting sex."

It is as if Typhoid Mary insisted upon her religious and civil right to work in the school cafeteria while complaining that the local health authorities were dragging their feet in coming up with a cure for her. Homosexuals should remember that any other communicable disease of the same seriousness as AIDS would be attacked with quarantine.

Homosexuals are proudly thumbing their noses at the God revealed to man in the Bible. We cannot know if the Creator would respond by punishing them with AIDS. But we cannot assume that He would not.

Even a man who was not a strong believer in God would have to conclude that the risk of AIDS teaches us about proper conduct in sexual activity.

**Typhoid Mary was a woman who spread typhoid fever to more than fifty persons while working as a New York City cook in the early 1900s. Why does the author compare her to homosexuals?**

**Do you agree or disagree with the author's conclusion? Why or why not?**

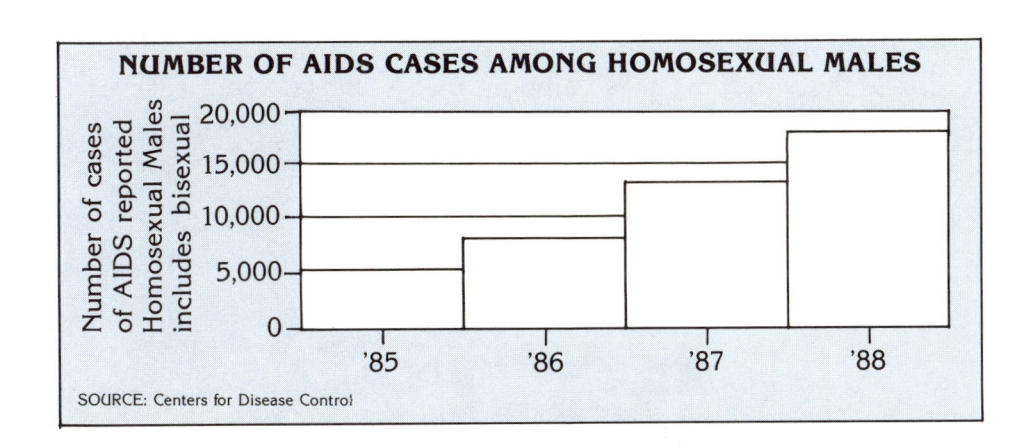

**NUMBER OF AIDS CASES AMONG HOMOSEXUAL MALES**

| Year | Number of cases |
|---|---|
| '85 | ~5,500 |
| '86 | ~8,500 |
| '87 | ~13,500 |
| '88 | ~18,500 |

Number of AIDS cases reported — Homosexual Males includes bisexual

SOURCE: Centers for Disease Control

---

**Is homosexuality immoral?**

How many facts does the author give to prove his view that homosexuality is immoral? List at least three opinions the author uses to support his argument.

Does the author suggest a way to control AIDS? If not, what do you think the author would suggest?

# VIEWPOINT 6 AIDS is not a moral issue

> **Editor's Note:** This viewpoint was paraphrased from an article by Alan M. Dershowitz, a professor at Harvard Law School. In it, Professor Dershowitz argues that people should be given scientific information about AIDS. Professor Dershowitz says this scientific information should be separated from the debate about whether homosexuality is moral or not.

**What evidence does the author offer to prove that people are exaggerating the risk of catching AIDS?**

It is time to take the moralism and politics out of the informational part of the AIDS debate.

The moralists and the politicians can continue to argue about how society should respond to AIDS. But let the flow of scientific information be unpolluted by people's opinions about how moral homosexuality is.

We have all heard exaggerated warnings about how easily AIDS is spread. Frightened parents who want to keep AIDS victims out of school and others who think that AIDS victims should be quarantined are both exaggerating the AIDS risk.

Harvard Professor William Haseltine, one of the leading scientists in AIDS research, is part of a team that has made some important discoveries about AIDS. He and a lot of other medical experts think that the small amount that is known about AIDS is being distorted by those who think homosexuality is immoral.

Scientists must not be influenced by the moralistic debate. They should consider the disease as if it were not spread by homosexual contact.

TIME RUNNING OUT FOR AIDS VICTIMS

26 JUNIORS

We should not listen to those who want to use AIDS to prove whether a particular lifestyle is moral or not. If the issue were whether eating pork caused a disease, we would not want Orthodox rabbis—who consider eating pork a sin—to decide the issue.

We have a right to know the hard facts about AIDS without moral judgments from either side. We need to hear more objective information about AIDS. Then each of us can make his/her own moral decision about what society should do as the AIDS epidemic spreads more widely.

**Why does the author compare AIDS moralists to Orthodox rabbis? Do you agree with his comparison? Why or why not?**

**Is the author arguing that AIDS is not a moral issue?**

### AIDS DEATHS
June 1981 through May 23, 1988

| Adults | Number | Percent |
| --- | --- | --- |
| Homosex/Bisex males | 21,661 | 61.6% |
| IV Drug Abusers | 9,127 | 26.0% |
| Heterosexuals | 1,358 | 3.9% |
| Hemophiliac/Coag. disorders | 357 | 1.0% |
| Transfusions | 1,032 | 2.9% |
| Unknown | 1,073 | 3.0% |
| **Children** | | |
| Parent with/at risk AIDS | 441 | 1.3% |
| Transfusion and other | 139 | 0.4% |
| **Total** | **35,188** | **100.0%** |

SOURCE: The Washington Times

### Morality and AIDS

The author thinks that the moral debate over AIDS should be separated from scientific research. How many facts does he give to prove his point? Name three opinions the author gives to support his view.

The author thinks AIDS research is being slowed down by those who have a moral side to take in the debate. Why does he think this? How do we decide who has a moral stake in the research and who does not? If you were a scientist, do you think you could separate your moral views from your work?

## CRITICAL THINKING SKILL 3
## Analyzing AIDS Advertising

More and more advertisements about AIDS are appearing in newspapers and magazines. Instead of selling a product, however, these advertisements attempt to educate people about the disease.

These advertisements deliver their messages in different ways. Some of these advertisements try to scare people into paying attention to the AIDS epidemic. Others offer factual information so people can become informed about how AIDS is spread. In this activity you will be examining two ads and analyzing the information each presents.

### PART I

Examine ad number one. What is the ad's message? Who are the people in the ad? What audience is this ad meant to appeal to? What facts about AIDS are included in the ad? As you read, is there any statement in particular that stands out? If so, is this statement a fact or an opinion?

### THE FACTS OF LIFE INCLUDE THE FACTS ABOUT AIDS.

AIDS is a fact of life for today's children. And that includes your kids.

You don't have to be a scientist to talk about AIDS with your children. All you have to be is what you are—a loving, concerned parent. But you do need to know the facts about AIDS. That it is not a homosexual disease. That it isn't spread through casual contact. Make sure your kids know the ways to protect themselves from the disease. Need more help? Call the Minnesota AIDSLine at 1-800-248-AIDS for immediate, accurate, private, and personalized information on what to tell your kids and how to go about doing it.

Talk to your children about AIDS—and keep talking to them about it. Because these days, not knowing everything about the facts of life could lead to an early death.

### Anyone Can Get AIDS. Everyone Can Prevent It.

©1987 The Minnesota AIDS Media Consortia.

Now look at ad number two. What is its message? How is the message different from the one presented in ad number one? How does the picture differ from the picture in ad number one? What audience is this ad meant to appeal to? What facts are presented in this ad? As you read, is there any statement in particular that stands out? If so, is this statement a fact or an opinion?

After looking at both ads, do you think one is more effective than the other? Why?

## PART II

Individually or in small groups, draw an AIDS ad. Include two facts that you have learned about AIDS in your ad.

**ONCE YOU HAVE AIDS, YOU HAVE IT TILL THE DAY YOU DIE.**

The bad news about AIDS is that everyone who gets it dies.

The good news is that you don't have to get it. AIDS *can* be prevented. How? Practice responsible sex. Say "no," or stick with one partner. If you have more than one partner, always use condoms.

Want to know more—about how *not* to get AIDS, the right way to use a condom, or how you can help stop AIDS? Personalized, confidential information is just a phone call away. Call the Minnesota AIDSLine at 1-800-248-AIDS.

*Anyone Can Get AIDS.
Everyone Can Prevent It.*

©1987 The Minnesota AIDS Media Consortia.

AIDS

# GLOSSARY OF TERMS

**AIDS**   Acquired Immune Deficiency Syndrome; a viral infection that causes a breakdown in the body's immune system. AIDS damages our body's natural ability to fight off disease.

**blood transfusion**   The transfer of blood into the vein of a person or animal.

**casual contact**   Non-sexual contact between people; includes being in the same room with, holding hands with, and providing medical care for a person.

**communicable disease**   A disease that can be passed from one person to another.

**confidentiality**   Assurance that certain knowledge or information will be kept secret.

**contagious**   The spread of a disease by contact with another person or object that may be contaminated with the disease.

**diagnose**   Deciding what disease a patient is suffering from by recognizing the signs of the disease; for example, a doctor could diagnose a cold by recognizing that the patient has a runny nose.

**experimental drugs**   Drugs that are being tested on animals and humans to determine whether they help or harm patients.

**gay**   See definition of homosexual.

**homosexual**   A person who prefers to have sex with a member of his or her own sex.

**immune system**   The part of the body that keeps a person healthy by destroying disease.

**incubation period**   The period of time between the infection of a person by a virus or germ and the appearance of the disease.

**infect**   To cause a person to become sick by transferring a germ or virus to him or her.

**intravenous**   Occurring in or entering through the blood stream; an intravenous drug user injects drugs into his or her veins.

**quarantine**   To keep a diseased person away from other people for a period of time in order to prevent the disease from spreading.

**vaccine**   A medication given to prevent illness.

AIDS   **31**